I CAN MAKE
MODELS

Author: Fiona Campbell

Illustrated by Michael Evans

Photography by Steve Shott

Series editor: Paula Borton

Series designer: Robert Walster

© 1996 Watts Books

Watts Books
96 Leonard Street
London EC2A 4RH

Franklin Watts Australia
14 Mars Road
Lane Cove
NSW 2066

ISBN (pbk): 0 7496 3259 3
ISBN (hbk): 0 7496 2038 2
Dewey Decimal Classification: 745.592

A CIP catalogue record for
this book is available from
the British Library.

Printed in Malaysia
10 9 8 7 6 5 4 3 2 1

Getting ready

Before you start, check that you have everything for your model-making. You can find most things around your home, anything else you can easily find in stationery shops. On the opposite page you can see general things you will need for making all the projects.

Be prepared

Before you begin, cover the area where you are working with paper. Wear an apron.

Try to keep your hands clean and wash them as soon as they get sticky or covered with paint.

Always wash your messy paintbrushes and don't forget to put the lids back onto felt-tip pens.

Be careful

Always be very careful when you use scissors. If you find anything tricky to cut, ask an adult to help you.

stick glue

paint

PVA glue

craft pipe-cleaners

round-ended scissors

ruler

pencils

paintbrushes

felt-tip pens

coloured paper

3

Tissue tortoise

You can use 2 shades of paper to decorate.

Open the box to pull out the tissues.

You will need:

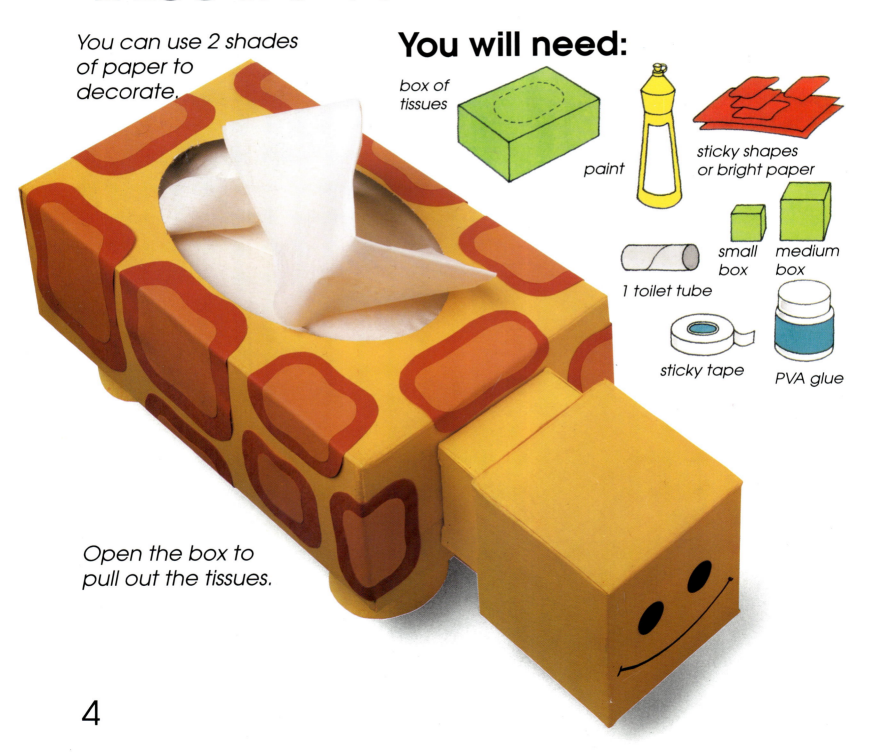

box of tissues

paint

sticky shapes or bright paper

1 toilet tube

small box

medium box

sticky tape

PVA glue

1.

Paint the boxes and the toilet tube all over in a bright colour.

2.

Cut the tube into four, and tape them to the bottom of the box.

3.

Glue the smaller boxes on one end to make a neck and head.

4.

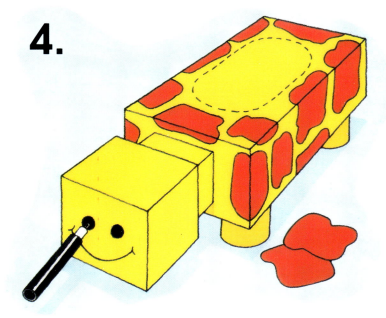

Stick on paper shapes. Draw on eyes and a mouth.

5

Monster mouth

You will need:

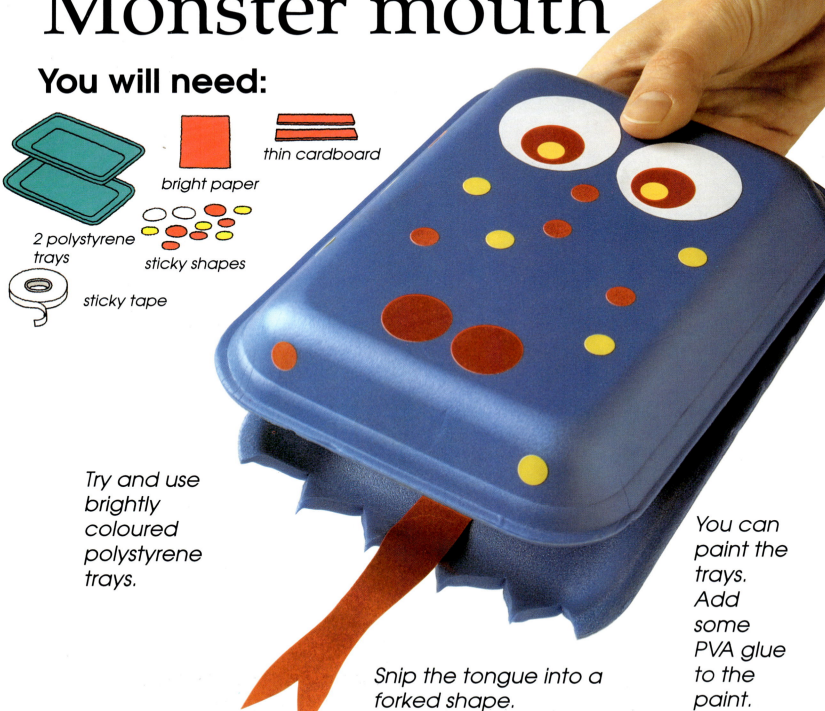

2 polystyrene trays

bright paper

thin cardboard

sticky shapes

sticky tape

Try and use brightly coloured polystyrene trays.

Snip the tongue into a forked shape.

You can paint the trays. Add some PVA glue to the paint.

6

1.

Cut zigzag teeth in a short edge of one of the trays. Be very careful as you cut.

2.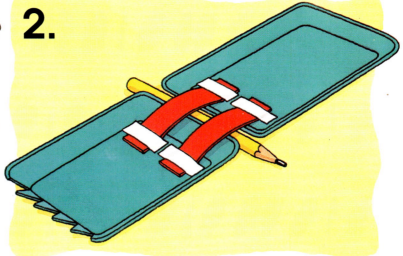

With the trays a pencil width apart, tape two strips of thin cardboard across the gap.

3.

Carefully bend one tray over so that the jaws close. Don't crease the cardboard.

4.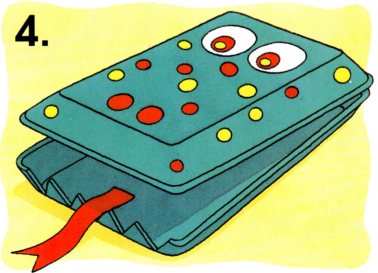

For eyes and a nose press sticky shapes onto the top tray. Tape on a dangling paper tongue.

Hovering bee

You will need:

plate

thread

black tissue paper

white paper

stick glue

yellow paper

paint

PVA glue

sticky shapes

pipe-cleaners

Hang up your bee with thread and watch it hover.

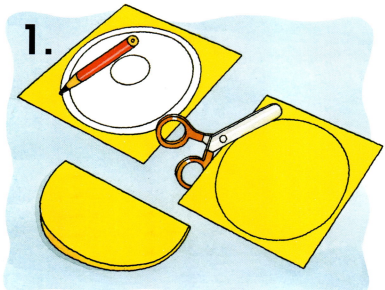

1.

Draw around the plate. Cut out the circle and fold it in half.

2.

Cut along the fold. Paint or draw lines around one half shape.

8

3.

Glue halfway and overlap the edge to make it into a cone.

4.

For the head, scrunch up a tissue paper ball and glue it in the cone.

5.

Bend some pipe-cleaners and glue them onto the cone.

6.

Cut and glue on paper wings. Add sticky shapes for eyes.

Rocking head

You will need:

2 paper plates

glue stick

paint

coloured paper

Stand your face up and see it rock.

Try making a clown face. Add paper hair instead of ears.

1.

Paint the bottom of both plates. Leave them to dry.

2.

Fold both plates in half. Crease each fold well. Open out again.

3.

Cut and glue on paper ear shapes.

4.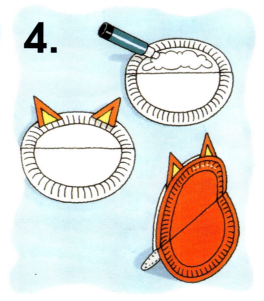

Glue the top halves of both plates together.

5.

Add paper eyes, nose and a mouth.

11

Greedy mice

You will need:

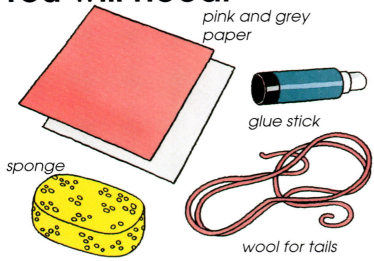

pink and grey paper

glue stick

sponge

wool for tails

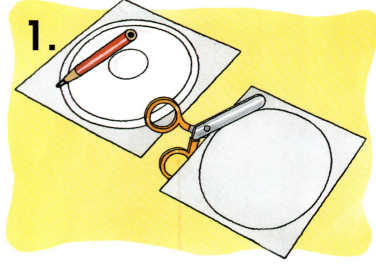

1. Draw around a saucer on grey paper. Cut out the circle.

2. Fold the circle. Then cut it in half. Each half will make a cone.

3. Glue along half the straight edge. Fold edges over to make a cone. Make as many cones as you like.

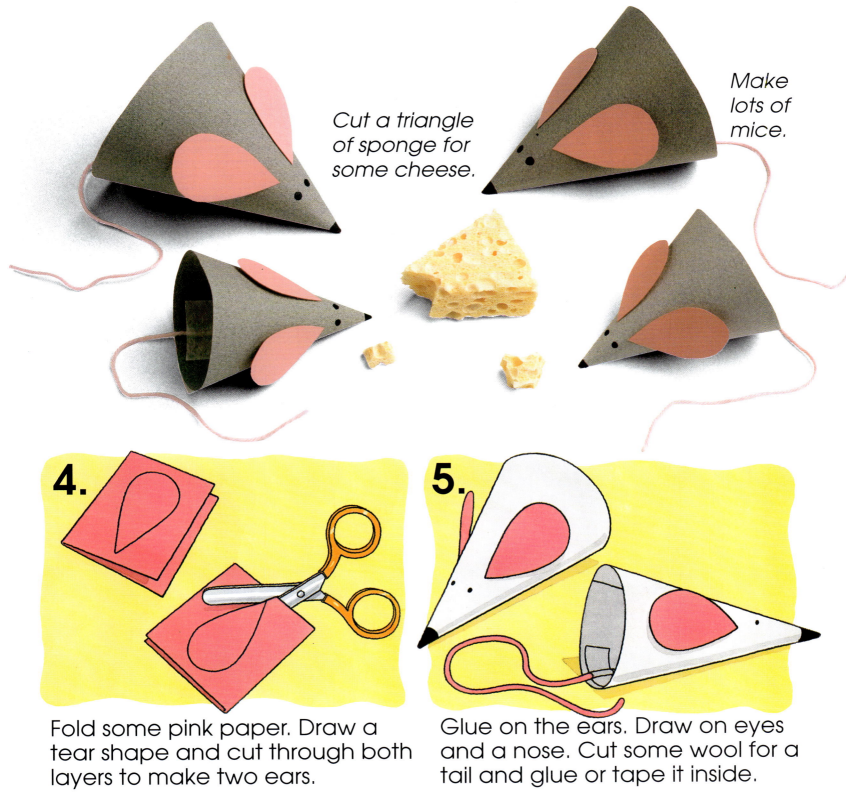

Cut a triangle of sponge for some cheese.

Make lots of mice.

4. Fold some pink paper. Draw a tear shape and cut through both layers to make two ears.

5. Glue on the ears. Draw on eyes and a nose. Cut some wool for a tail and glue or tape it inside.

13

Sunflower

You will need:

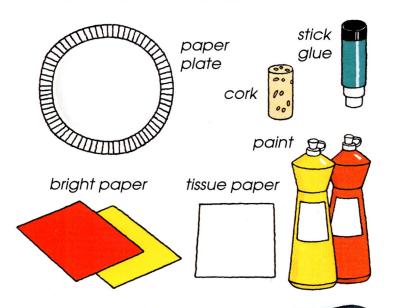

paper plate

cork

stick glue

paint

bright paper

tissue paper

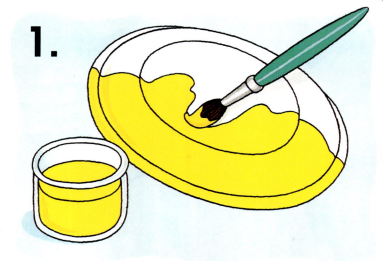

1.

Turn the plate over and paint the bottom in a bright colour.

2.

Print lots of circles with the cork in the middle of the plate.

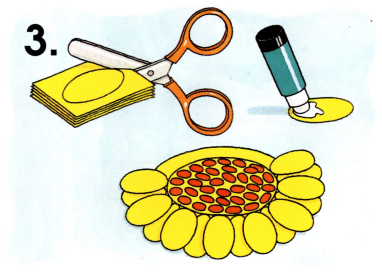

3.

Cut lots of paper petals and glue them around the edge.

14

4.

Cut out some yellow and red insect shapes. Decorate them.

5.

Glue on tissue paper wings. Stick insects all over the flower.

You can stick your flower on a window.

15

Jolly tube man

You will need:

toilet tube

stick glue

bright paper

sticky shapes

saucer

sticky tape

thin card

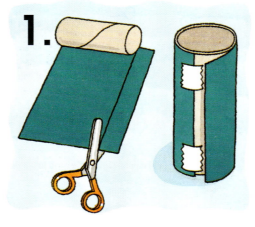

1.

Cut a piece of bright paper and tape it around the toilet tube.

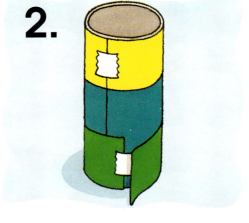

2.

Cut two thinner strips and tape those around the tube too.

3.

For arms and legs, roll paper around a fat pen. Tape it then slide the pen out.

4.

Draw and cut out hands and feet using brightly coloured thin card.

5.

Pinch one end of each arm and leg and glue on. Add hands and feet.

6.

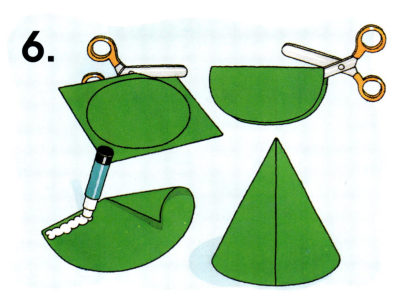

For a hat, draw around a saucer. Cut out the circle. Cut it in half and bend it to make a cone.

7.

Add the hat. Then decorate your tube man with sticky shapes.

You can make a whole family of tube people.

You can decorate your tube man with paint or felt-tip pens instead of sticky shapes.

17

Tight snake

You can use red and white paper circles for eyes.

You will need:

a bright pair of old tights

PVA glue

newspaper

elastic bands

sponge cloths

red paper

You can use coloured felt for decoration if you have some.

1.

Cut one leg off the tights. Scrunch up a sheet of newspaper into a sausage shape. Make lots.

2.

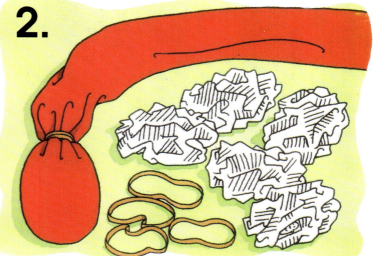

Push a paper sausage right into the foot. Wrap an elastic band tightly around the end.

3.

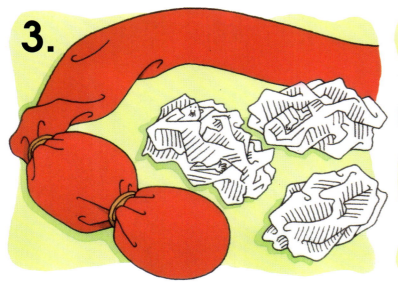

Put another scrunched up sausage shape inside. Then add another elastic band.

4.

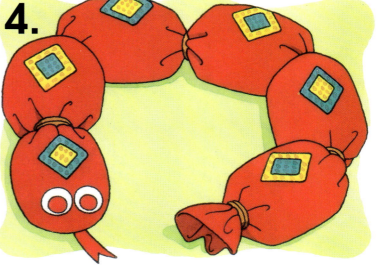

Carry on until you reach the end. Glue on a red tongue, eyes and sponge shapes along its back.

See-through shuttle

You will need:

Clean, dry plastic bottle

bright paper

foil

tape

sticky shapes

card

thread

small piece of card for astronaut.

1.

For the wings, lay the bottle onto the cardboard and draw a triangle as shown in the picture.

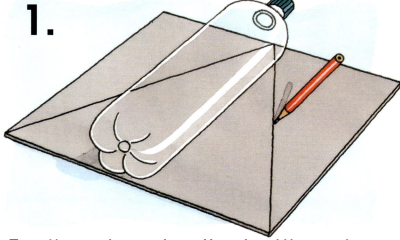

2.

Carefully cut out the triangle and tape it to the bottle in two places.

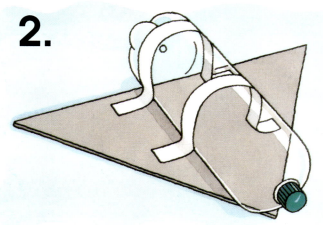

3.

Draw and cut out an astronaut. Cover it in foil and pencil on a helmet and boots. Tape on thread.

You can glue a sponge cloth space pack on your astronaut.

Decorate the shuttle with brightly coloured tape if you like.

4.

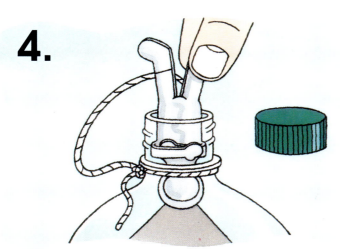

Tie the thread end around the top of the bottle. Bend the astronaut to put it inside.

5.

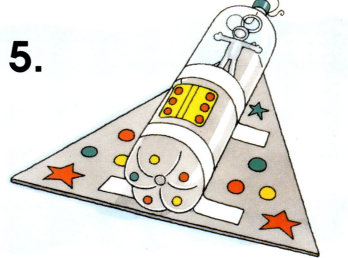

Screw on the lid. Decorate the shuttle with bright paper and sticky shapes.

21

Money-box robot

You will need:

empty tissue box

small box

paint

2 toothpaste boxes

small margarine tub with lid

2 toilet tubes

2 pipe-cleaners

PVA glue

1.

Get an adult to cut a coin-sized slit in the top end of the margarine tub.

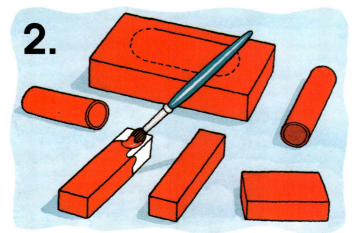

2.

Paint the boxes and the toilet tubes all over in a bright colour. Leave to dry.

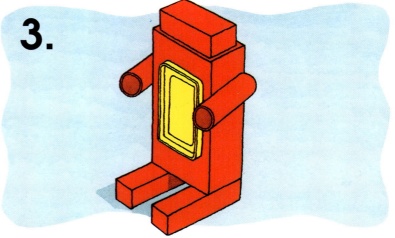

3.

Glue on the head, legs and arms to the tissue box. Add the lid of the tub to the robot's tummy.

4.

Curl the pipe-cleaners around a pencil. Pull them off and push them into the head.

5.

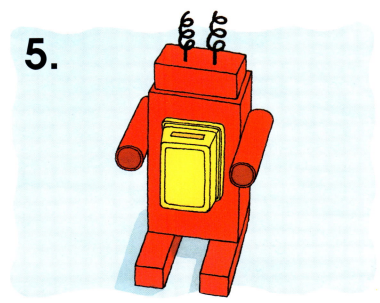

Push the margarine tub onto the robot's tummy with the slit at the top.

Decorate the body with sticky shapes or glue on paper ones. Add big eyes.

Undersea world

You will need:

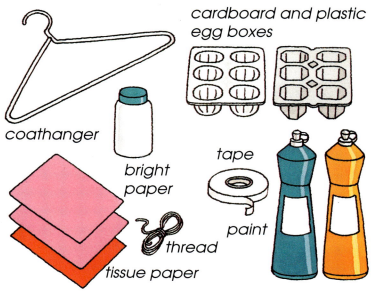

coathanger

bright paper

tissue paper

thread

cardboard and plastic egg boxes

tape

paint

1. *Watch out! The plastic ones are sharp.*

Cut all the sections from the egg boxes. Paint and decorate the cardboard ones.

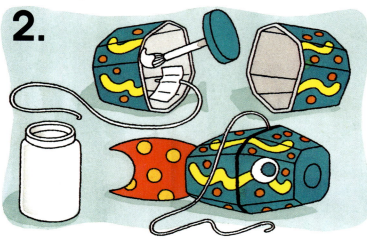

2.

Tape thread inside one bit. Glue another section to it to make a fish. Add a paper tail and eyes.

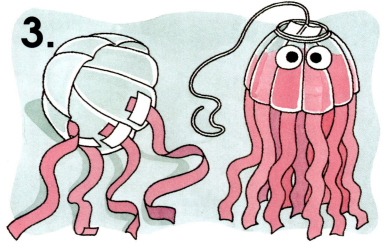

3.

For a jellyfish, glue strips of tissue paper into a plastic bit. Add eyes and thread.

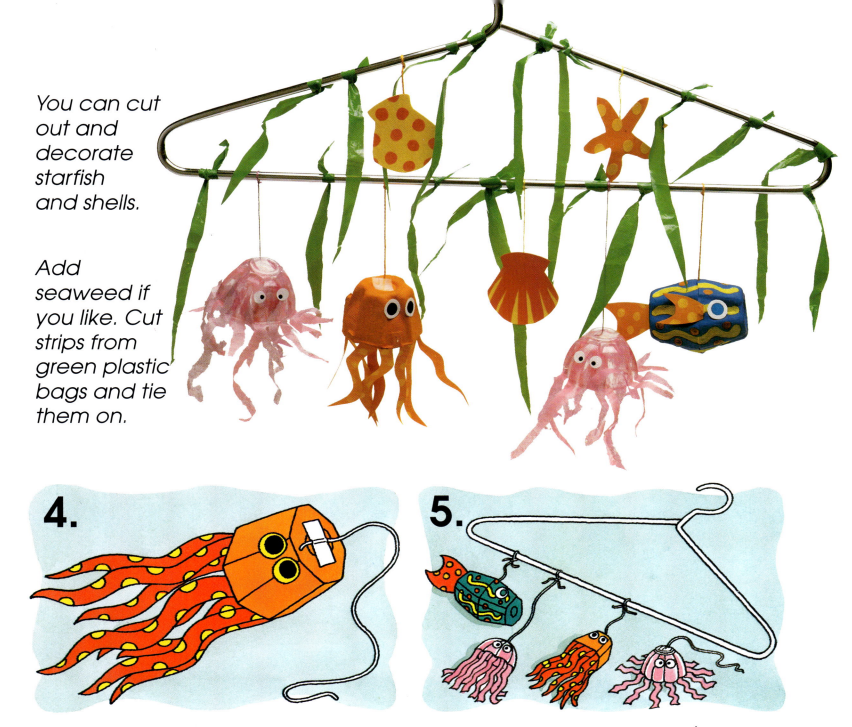

You can cut out and decorate starfish and shells.

Add seaweed if you like. Cut strips from green plastic bags and tie them on.

4. Add eight paper legs for an octopus. Tape thread to the top. Add eyes.

5. Make as many sea creatures as you like. Tie them to the coathanger.

Curly conebird

You will need:

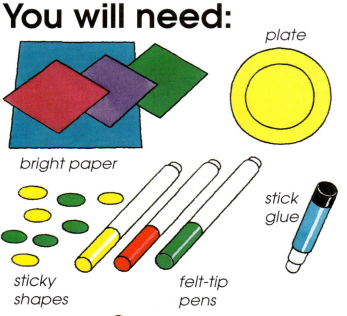

plate

bright paper

sticky shapes

felt-tip pens

stick glue

1.

Draw around the plate. Cut out the circle. Fold it and cut along the fold. You only need one half.

2.

Glue halfway along the straight edge. Overlap the edges and press hard to make a cone.

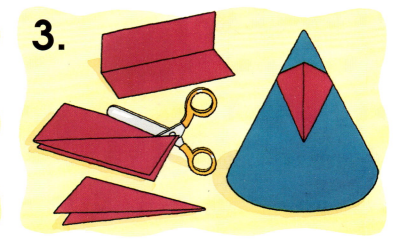

3.

Fold a paper rectangle and draw a line across it. Cut along the line. Glue it on for a beak.

4.

Cut one strip of paper for a tail and two for wings. Make lots of thin cuts. Cut two feet shapes.

5.

Roll the wings and tail around a pencil to curl the ends. Glue on the wings, tail and feet.

You can add a crest. Make it the same way as the tail. Glue it on behind its head.

Decorate your bird with felt-tip pens and sticky shapes.

Fish fingers

Slide your hand inside and make your fish swim.

You will need:

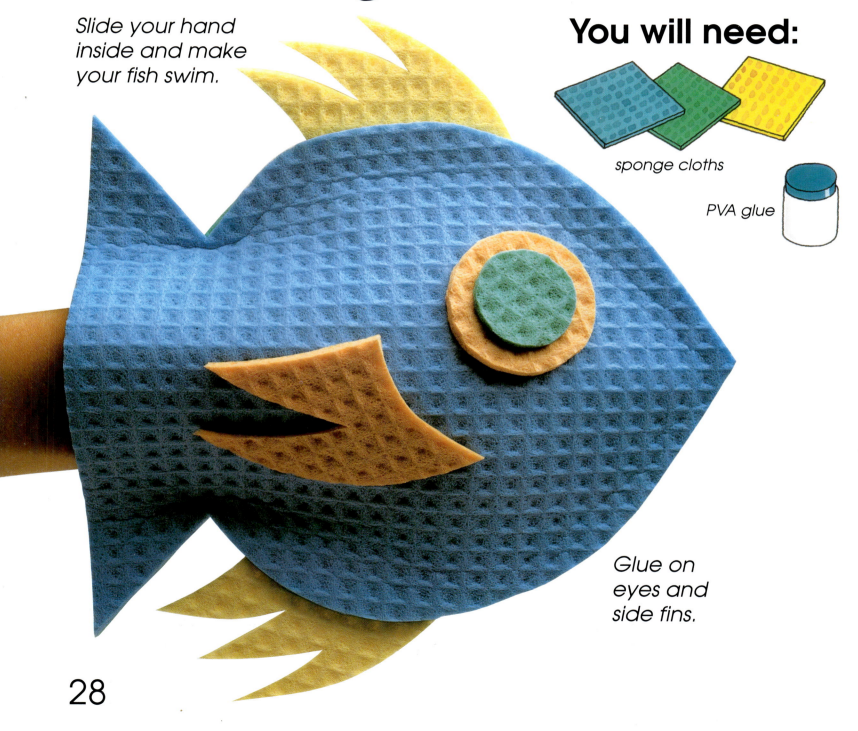

sponge cloths

PVA glue

Glue on eyes and side fins.

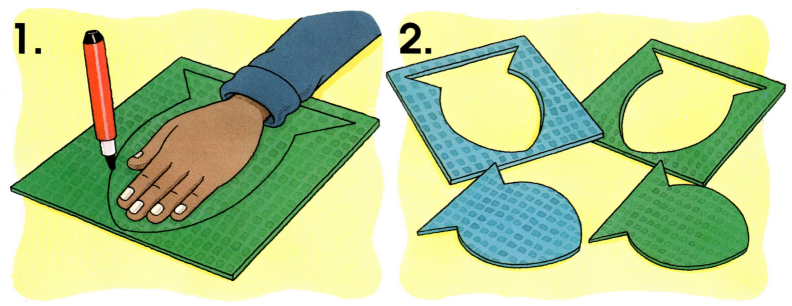

1. Put your hand and wrist on one of the cloths. Draw a fish shape around it.

2. Cut out the fish. Draw around it onto another cloth and cut out a second fish.

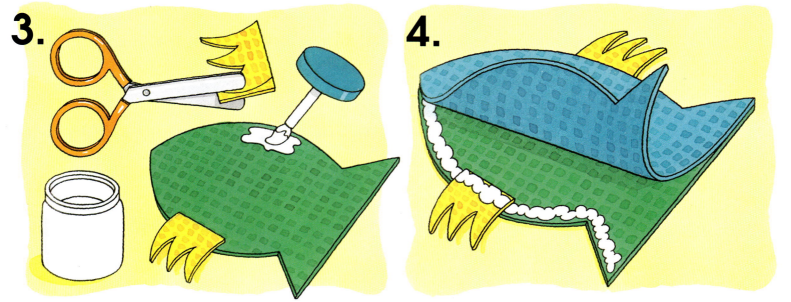

3. Cut out spiky fins. Glue them onto one fish shape.

4. Glue one fish, leaving the end free. Press the other on top.

29

Racing car

You will need:

1 large cardboard fruit box

paint

PVA glue

tape

5 paper plates

large piece of cardboard

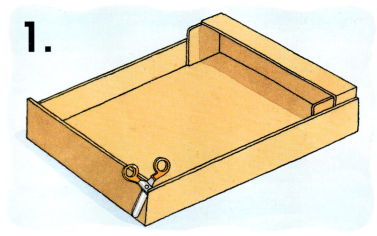

1.

Get someone to help you to cut down both sides of one end of the box.

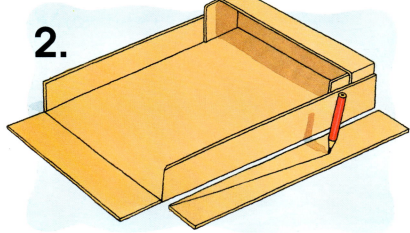

2.

Cut some card the same size as the side of the box. Draw a line across it as in the picture above.

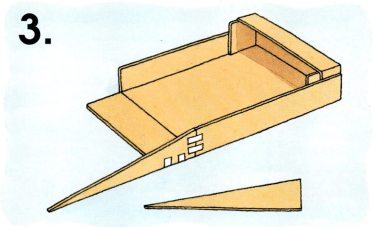

3.

Cut along the diagonal line. Tape each piece onto the front of the box.

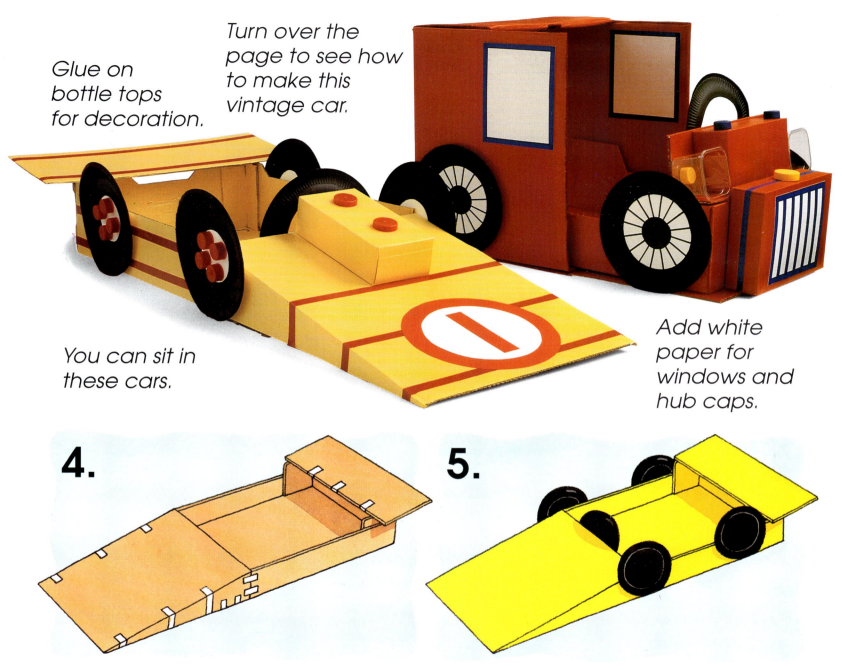

Glue on bottle tops for decoration.

Turn over the page to see how to make this vintage car.

You can sit in these cars.

Add white paper for windows and hub caps.

4.

Cut another piece of card to fit on top. Tape it on. Add a spoiler on the back.

5.

Paint and glue on the wheels and a steering wheel. Paint and decorate your car.

31

Vintage car

You will need:

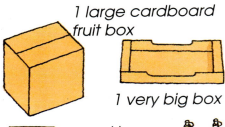
1 large cardboard fruit box

1 very big box

cereal box

paint

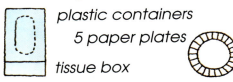
plastic containers

5 paper plates

tissue box

1.
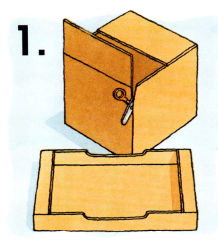
Get someone to help you cut one end of the big box and the fruit box.

2.
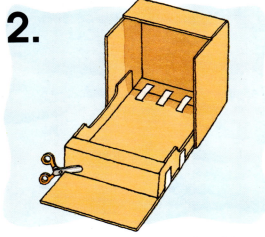
Tape the fruit box half inside the other box. Cut off the spare cardboard at the front.

3.

Tape on the spare piece of cardboard at the front as a windshield.

4.
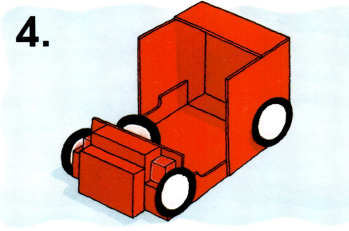
Glue on the other boxes. Add headlamps, wheels and a steering wheel. Paint your car.